Introduction by W. Terrence Gordon

This piece, reprinted from the *University of Windsor Review*, Vol. 11, No. 1, Fall, 1966, pages 1-10, deals with *formal cause*, without once using this phrase. It is hinted at playful in the reference to the legend of Humpty-Dumpty, that "would seem to suggest a parallel to the 10%-90% distribution of causes and effects" — a reference to the statistic used by McLuhan in his opening paragraph. The formal of formal cause is also echoed deliberately in the numerous references to *forms* and *transformations*, whether of language, nature, music, painting, or poetry. It is also echoed in *information* and thus gives McLuhan a subtle rhetorical device for focusing on his theme: "In the age of information, it is information itself that becomes environmental." Mining the work of all artists since the advent of electricity for the anti-environmental awareness they intuitively provide is the cornerstone of McLuhan's implicit program of educational reform. — WTG

The Relation of Environment to Anti-Environment

Under the heading that "What exists is likely to be misallocated" Peter Drucker in *Managing for Results* discusses the structure of social situations. "Business enterprise is not a phenomenon of nature but one of society. In a social situation, however, events are not distributed according to the 'normal distribution' of a natural universe (that is, they are not distributed according to the bell-shaped Gaussian curve). In a social situation a very small number of events *at one extreme* — the first 10 per cent to 20 per cent at most — account for 90 per cent of all results; whereas the great majority of events accounts for 10 per cent or so of the results." What Drucker is presenting here is the environment as it presents itself for human attention and action. He is confronting the phenomenon of the imperceptibility of the environment as such. It is this factor that Edward T. Hall also tackles in *The Silent Language.* The ground rules, the pervasive structure, the overall pattern eludes perception except in so far as there is an anti-environment or a counter-situation constructed to provide a means of direct attention. Paradoxically, the 10 per cent of the typical situation that Drucker designates as the area of effective cause and as the area of opportunity, this small factor is the environment. The 90 per cent area is the area of problems generated by the active power of the 10 per cent environment. For the environment is an active process pervading and impinging upon all the components of the situation. It is easy to illustrate this.

Any new technology, any extension or amplification of human faculties when given material embodiment, tends to create a new environment. This is as true of clothing as of speech, or script, or wheel. This process is more easily observed in our own time when several new environments have been created. To take only the latest one, TV, we find a handful of engineers and technicians in the 10 per cent area, as it were, creating a set of radical changes in the 90 per cent area of daily life. The new TV environment is an electric circuit that takes as its content the earlier environment, the photograph and the movie in particular. It is in the interplay between the old and the new environments that there is generated an innumerable series of problems and confusions. They extend all the way from how to allocate the time of children and adults to the problem of pay-TV and TV in the classroom. The new medium of TV as an environment creates new occupations. As an environment, it is imperceptible except in terms of its content. That is, all that is seen or noticed is the old environment, the movie. But even the effects of TV on the movie go unnoticed, and the effects of the TV environment in altering the entire character of human sensibility and sensory ratios is completely ignored.

The content of any system or organization naturally consists of the preceding system or organization, and in that degree acts as a control on the new environment. It is useful to notice all of the arts and sciences as acting in the role of anti-environments that enable us to perceive the environment. In a business civilization we have long considered liberal study as providing necessary means of orientation and perception. When the arts and sciences themselves become environments under conditions of electric circuitry, conventional liberal studies whether in the arts or sciences will no longer serve as an anti-environment. When we live in a museum without walls, or have music as a structural part of our sensory environment, new strategies of attention and perception have to be created. When the highest scientific knowledge creates the environment of the atom bomb, new controls for the scientific environment have to be discovered, if only in the interest of survival.

The structural examples of the relation of environment to anti-environment need to be multiplied as a means of understanding the principles of perception and activity involved. The Balinese say: "We have no art—we do everything as well as possible." This is not an ironic but a merely factual remark. In a preliterate society art serves as a means of merging the individual and the environment, not as a means of training perception upon the environment. Archaic or primitive art looks to us like a magical control built into the environment. Thus to put the artefacts from such a culture into a museum or anti-environment is an act of nullification rather than of revelation. Today what is called "Pop Art" is the use of some object in our own daily environment as if it were anti-environmental. Pop Art serves to remind us, however, that we have fashioned for ourselves a world of artefacts and images that are intended not to train perception or awareness but to insist that we merge with them as the primitive man merges with his environment. The world of modern advertising is a magical environment constructed to produce effects for the total economy but not designed to increase human awareness. We have designed schools as anti-environments to develop the perception and judgment of the printed word. There are no means of training provided to develop similar perception and judgment of any of the new environments created by electric circuitry. This is not accidental. From the development of phonetic script until the invention of the electric telegraph human technology had tended strongly towards the furtherance of detachment and objectivity, detribalization and individuality. Electric circuitry has quite the contrary effect. It involves in depth. It merges the individual and the mass environment. To create an anti-environment for such electric technology would seem to require a technological extension of consciousness itself. The awareness and opposition of the individual are in these circumstances as irrelevant as they are futile.

The structural features of environment and anti-environment appear in the age-old clash between professionalism and amateurism, whether in sport or in studies. Professional sport is environmental and amateur sport is anti-environmental. Professional sport fosters the merging of the individual in the mass and in the patterns of the total environment. Amateur sport seeks rather the development of critical awareness of the individual and most of all, critical awareness of the ground rules of the society as such. The same contrast exists for studies. The professional tends to specialize and to merge his being uncritically in the mass. The ground rules provided by the mass response of his colleagues serve as a pervasive environment of which he is uncritical and unaware.

The party system of government affords a familiar image of the relations of environment and anti-environment. The government as environment needs the opposition as anti-environment in order to be aware of itself. The role of the opposition would seem to be that of the arts and sciences in creating perception. As the government environment becomes more cohesively involved in a world of instant information, opposition would seem to become increasingly necessary but also intolerable. Opposition begins to assume the rancorous and hostile character of a Dew Line, or a Distant Early Warning System. It is important, however, to consider the role of the arts and sciences as Early Warning Systems in the social environment. The models of perception provided in the arts and sciences alike can serve as indispensable means of orientation to future problems well before they become troublesome.

The legend of Humpty-Dumpty would seem to suggest a parallel to the 10%-90% distribution of causes and effects. The impact that resulted in his fall brought into play a massive response from the social bureaucracy. But all the King's horses and all the King's men could not put Humpty-Dumpty back together again. They could not recreate the old environment, they could only create a new one. Our typical response to a disrupting new technology is to recreate the old environment instead of heeding the new opportunities of the new environment. Failure to notice the new opportunities is also failure to understand the new powers. This means that we fail to develop the necessary controls or anti-environments for the new environment. This failure leaves us in the role of automata merely.

W. T. Easterbrook has done extensive exploration of the relations of bureaucracy and enterprise, discovering that as soon as one becomes the environment, the other becomes an anti-environment. They seem to bicycle along through history alternating their roles with all the dash and vigor of tweedle-dum and tweedle-dee. In the 18th century when *realism* became a new method in literature, what happened was that the external environment was put in the place of anti-environment. The ordinary world was given the role of art object by Daniel Defoe and others. The environment began to be used as a perceptual probe. It became self-conscious. It became an "anxious object" instead of being an unperceived and pervasive pattern. Environment used as probe or art object is satirical because it draws attention to itself. The romantic poets extended this technique to external nature transforming nature into an art object. Beginning with Baudelaire and Rimbaud and continuing in Hopkins and Eliot and James Joyce, the poets turned their attention to language as a probe. Long used as an environment, language became an instrument of exploration and research. It became an anti-environment. It became Pop Art.

The artist as a maker of anti-environments permits us to perceive that much is newly environmental and therefore most active in transforming situations. This would seem to be why the artist has in many circles in the past century been called the enemy, the criminal. It helps to explain why news has a natural bias toward crime and bad news. It is this kind of news that enables us to perceive our world. The detective since Poe's Dupin has tended to be a probe, an artist of the big town, an artist-enemy, as it were. Conventionally, society is always one phase back, is never environmental. Paradoxically, it is the antecedent environment that is always being upgraded for our attention. The new environment always uses the old environment as its material.

In the Spring issue of the *Varsity Grad* (1965) Glenn Gould discusses the effects of recorded music on performance and composition. One of his main points is that as recorded music creates a new environment the audience in effect becomes participant both in performance and in composition. This is a reversal or chiasmus of form that occurs in any situation where an environment is pushed up into high intensity or high definition by technological change. A reversal of characteristics occurs as in the case with bureaucracy and enterprise. An environment is naturally of low intensity or low definition. That is why it escapes observation. Anything that raises the environment to high intensity, whether it be a storm in nature or violent change resulting from a new technology, such high intensity turns the environment into an object of attention. When an environment becomes an object of attention it assumes the character of an anti-environment or an art object. When the social environment is stirred up to exceptional intensity by technological change and becomes a focus of much attention, we apply the terms "war" and "revolution." All the components of "war" are present in any environment whatever. The recognition of war depends upon their being stepped up to high definition.

Under electric conditions of instant information movement both the concept and the reality of war become manifest in many of the situations of daily life. We have long been accustomed to war as that which goes on between publics or nations. Publics and nations were the creation of print technology. With electric circuitry the publics and nations became the content of the new technology: "The mass audience is not a public as environment but a public as content of a new electric environment." And whereas "the public" as an environment created by print technology consisted of separate individuals with varying points of view, the mass audience consists of the same individuals involved in depth in one another and involved in the creative process of the art or educational situation that is presented to them. Art and education were presented to the *public* as consumer packages for their instruction and edification. The new mass audience is involved immediately in art and education as participants and co-creators rather than as consumers. Art and education become new forms of experience, new environments, rather than new anti-environments. Pre-electric art and education were anti-environments in the sense that they were the content of various environments. Under electric conditions the content tends however towards becoming environmental itself. This was the paradox that Malraux found in The *Museum Without Walls*, and that Glenn Gould finds in recorded music. Music in the concert hall had been an anti-environment. The same music when recorded is *music without halls*, as it were.

Another paradoxical aspect of this change is that when music becomes environmental by electric means, it becomes more and more the concern of the private individual. By the same token and complementary to the same paradox the pre-electric music of the concert hall (the music when there was a public instead of a mass audience) was a corporate ritual for the group rather than the individual. This paradox extends to all electrical technology whatever. The same means which permit, for example, a universal and centralized thermostat do in effect encourage a private thermostat for individual manipulation. The age of the mass audience is thus far more individualistic than the preceding age of the *public*. It is this paradoxical dynamic that confuses every issue about "conformity" today and "separatism" and "integration." Profoundly contradictory actions and directions prevail in all of these situations. This is not surprising in an age of circuitry succeeding the age of the wheel. The feedback loop plays all sorts of tricks to confound the single plane and one-way direction of thought and action as they had been constituted in the pre-electric age of the machine.

Applying the above to the Negro question, one could say that the agrarian South has long tended to regard the Negro as environmental. As such, the Negro is a challenge, a threat, a burden. The very phrase "white supremacy" quite as much as the phrase "white trash" registers this environmental attitude. The environment is the enemy that must be subdued. To the rural man the conquest of Nature is an unceasing challenge. It is the Southerner who contributed the cowboy to the frontier. The Virginian, the archetypal cowboy as it were, confronts the environment as a hostile, natural force. To man on the frontier, other men are environmental and hostile. By contrast, to the townsman, men appear not as environmental, but as content of the urban environment.

Parallel to the Negro question is the French Canada problem. The English Canadians have been the environment of French Canada since the railway and Confederation. However, since the telegraph and radio and television, French Canada and English Canada alike have become the content of this new technology. Electric technology is totally environmental for all human communities today. Hence the great confusion arising from the transformation of environments into anti-environments, as it were. All the earlier groupings that had constituted separate environments before electricity have now become anti-environments or the content of the new technology. As such, the old unconscious environments tend to become increasingly centres of acute awareness. The content of any new environment is just as unperceived as the old one had been initially. As a merely automatic sequence, the succession of environments and of the dramatics thereto appertaining, tend to be rather tiresome, if only because the audience is very prone to participate in the dramatics with an enthusiasm proportioned to its unawareness. In the electric age all former environments whatever become anti-environments. As such, the old environments are transformed into areas of self-awareness and self-assertion, guaranteeing a very lively interplay of forces.

Eric Havelock in his book *Preface to Plato* has clarified the stages by which the written word served to detribalize the Greek world. After the tribal encyclopedia of oral and memorized wisdom, writing enabled man to organize knowledge by categories and classifications; what Plato called the *ideas*. With the origin of classified data, or visual organization of knowledge, there came also representation in the arts. Representation is itself a form of matching or classifying, unknown to preliterate or native artists. Today we return to non-objective art, non-representational art, because in the electric age we are leaving the world of visual organization of experience.

The visual sense, alone of our senses, creates the forms of space and time that are uniform, continuous and connected. Euclidean space is the prerogative of visual and literate man. With the advent of electric circuitry and the instant movement of information, Euclidean space recedes and the non-Euclidean geometries emerge. Lewis Carroll, the Oxford mathematician, was perfectly aware of this change in our world when he took Alice through the looking glass into the world where each object creates its own space and conditions. To the visual or Euclidean man, objects do not create time and space. They are merely fitted into time and space. The idea of the world as an environment that is more or less fixed, is very much the product of literacy and visual assumptions. In his book, *The Philosophical Impact of Contemporary Physics* Milič Čapek explains some of the strange confusions in the scientific mind that result from the encounter of the old non-Euclidean spaces of preliterate man with the Euclidean and Newtonian spaces of literate man. The scientists of our time are just as confused as the philosophers, or the teachers, and it is for the reason that Whitehead assigned; they still have the illusion that the new developments are to be fitted into the old space or environment.

One of the most obvious areas of change in the arts of our time has not only been the dropping of representation, but the dropping of the story line. In poetry, in the novel, in the movie, narrative continuity has yielded to thematic variation. Such variation in place of story line or melodic line has always been the norm in native societies. It is now becoming the norm in our own society and for the same reason, namely that we are becoming a non-visual society.

In the age of circuitry, or feedback, fragmentation and specialism tend to yield to integral forms of organization. Humpty-Dumpty tends to go back together again. The bureaucratic efforts of all the King's horses and all the King's men were naturally calculated to keep Humpty-Dumpty from ever getting together again. The Neolithic age, the age of the planter after the age of the hunter, was an age of specialism and division of labour. It has reached a somewhat startling terminus with the advent of electric circuitry. Circuitry is a profoundly decentralizing process. Paradoxically, it was the wheel and mechanical innovation that created centralism. The circuit reverses the characteristics of the wheel, just as Xerography reverses the characteristics of the printing press. Before printing, the scribe, the author, and the reader tended to merge. With printing, author and publisher became highly specialized and centralized forms of action. With Xerography, author, and publisher, and reader tend to merge once more. Whereas the printed book had been the first mass-produced product, creating uniform prices and markets, Xerography tends to restore the custom-made book. Writing and publishing tend to become services of a corporate and inclusive kind. The printed word created the Public. The Public consists of separate individuals, each with his own point of view. Electric circuitry does not create a Public. It creates the Mass. The Mass does not consist of separate individuals, but of individuals profoundly involved in one another. This involvement is a function, not of numbers, but of speed. The daily newspaper is an interesting example of this fact. The items in the daily press are totally discontinuous and totally unconnected. The only unifying feature of the press is the date line. Through that date line the reader must go, as Alice went, 'through the looking glass.' If it is not today's date line, he cannot get in. Once he goes through the date line, he is involved in a world of items for which he, the reader, must write a story line. He makes the news, as the reader of a detective story makes the plot.

Just as the printed press created the Public as a new environment, so does each new technology or extension of our physical powers tend to create new environments. In the age of information, it is information itself that becomes environmental. The satellites and antennae projected from our planet, for example, have transformed the planet from being an environment into being a probe. This is a transformation which the artists of the past century have been explaining to us in their endless experimental models. Modern art, whether in painting, or poetry, or music, began as a probe and not as a package. The Symbolists literally broke up the old packages and put them into our hands as probes. And whereas the package belongs to a consumer age, the probe belongs to an age of experimenters.

One of the peculiarities of art is to serve as an anti-environment, a probe that makes the environment visible. It is a form of symbolic, or parabolic, action. Parable means literally "to throw against," just as symbol means "to throw together." As we equip the planet with satellites and antennae, we tend to create new environments of which the planet is itself the content. It is peculiar to environments that they are complex processes which transform their content into archetypal forms. As the planet becomes the content of a new information environment, it also tends to become a work of art. Where railway and machine created a new environment for agrarian man, the old agrarian world became an art form. Nature became a work of art. The Romantic movement was born. When the electric circuit went around the mechanical environment, the machine itself became a work of art. Abstract art was born.

As information becomes our environment, it becomes mandatory to program the environment itself as a work of art. The parallel to this appears in Jacques Ellul's *Propaganda* where he sees propaganda, not as an ideology or content of any medium, but as the operation of all the media at once. The mother tongue is propaganda because it exercises an effect on all the senses at once. It shapes our entire outlook and our ways of feeling. Like any other environment, its operation is imperceptible. When an environment is new, we perceive the old one for the first time. What we see on the late show is not TV, but old movies. When the Emperor appeared in his new clothes, his courtiers did not see his nudity, they saw his old clothes. Only the small child and the artist have that immediacy of approach that permits perception of the environmental. The artist provides us with anti-environments that enable us to see the environment. Such anti-environmental means of perception must constantly be renewed in order to be efficacious. That basic aspect of the human condition by which we are rendered incapable of perceiving the environment is one to which psychologists have not even referred. In an age of accelerated change, the need to perceive the environment becomes urgent. Acceleration also makes such perception of the environment more possible. Was it not Bertrand Russell who said that if the bath water got only half a degree warmer every hour, we would never know when to scream? New environments reset our sensory thresholds. These in turn, alter our outlook and expectations.

The need of our time is for the means of measuring sensory thresholds and of discovering exactly what changes occur in these thresholds as a result of the advent of any particular technology. With such knowledge in hand, it would be possible to program a reasonable and orderly future for any human community. Such knowledge would be the equivalent of a thermostatic control for room temperatures. It would seem only reasonable to extend such controls to all the sensory thresholds of our being. We have no reason to be grateful to those who juggle the thresholds in the name of haphazard innovation.

The Relation of Environment to Anti-Environment
Marshall McLuhan - Unbound (04)

ISBN: 1-58423-051-7
Library of Congress Control Number 2005927213

Marshall McLuhan Unbound Project Editors
Eric McLuhan, W. Terrence Gordon

Published in United States in October 2005 by
Gingko Press, Inc.
5768 Paradise Drive, Suite J • Corte Madera, CA 94925
(415) 924-9615 • Fax (415) 924-9608
email: books@gingkopress.com
http://www.gingkopress.com

Design, packaging and production: Die Gestalten Verlag, Berlin
Layout and Typography: onlab, Berlin
Fonts: *Dolly* by Underware, *Bullet* by House Industries
Production: Martin Bretschneider, Vinzenz Geppert
Art direction: Robert Klanten

Made in Germany